To sign up for new releases and promotions, please visit www.kidzsynergy.com
Copyright © 2020 by Czarina Tran-Bernett
ISBN: 978-1-7333618-6-6

KidZ Synergy

"Liam," shouted Livy, "I heard mom talk to Aunt Shari on the phone. She sounded worried."

"We visited Aunt Shari, Uncle Mike, and cousin Kenzie last week," shrugged Liam.

Livy urgently responded, "I heard them say Uncle Mike is being tested for Covid-19."

"Oh No!"

"Is Kenzie also sick?" Liam asked.

"I don't know. She wasn't sick last week. What is COVID-19 anyway?" asked Livy.

"I'm not sure," answered Liam.

"Daddy's Home! Daddy, Mom said Uncle Mike is being tested for COVID-19." Livy said quickly.

Mom stood at the doorway and added, "I didn't want to worry you, so I didn't text message you."
"Daddy, Daddy," both Liam and Livy clamored, "What is COVID-19?"

Daddy explained, "COVID-19 is a new coronavirus. COVID-19 spreads very fast. It spreads through droplets when a person coughs, sneezes, sings, or talks. The virus can live on surfaces for days and it can stay in the air for hours.

Liam asked, "How does COVID-19 affect the human body?"

Daddy responded, "When it enters the human body, through the nose, mouth, or eyes, the virus attaches itself to a cell and quickly multiplies. It tells the human cell to make more bad viruses. When the infected cell becomes too full, it explodes, releasing the harmful viruses into the body and making us sick."

Livy glanced at Mom, "How is Uncle Mike doing?"

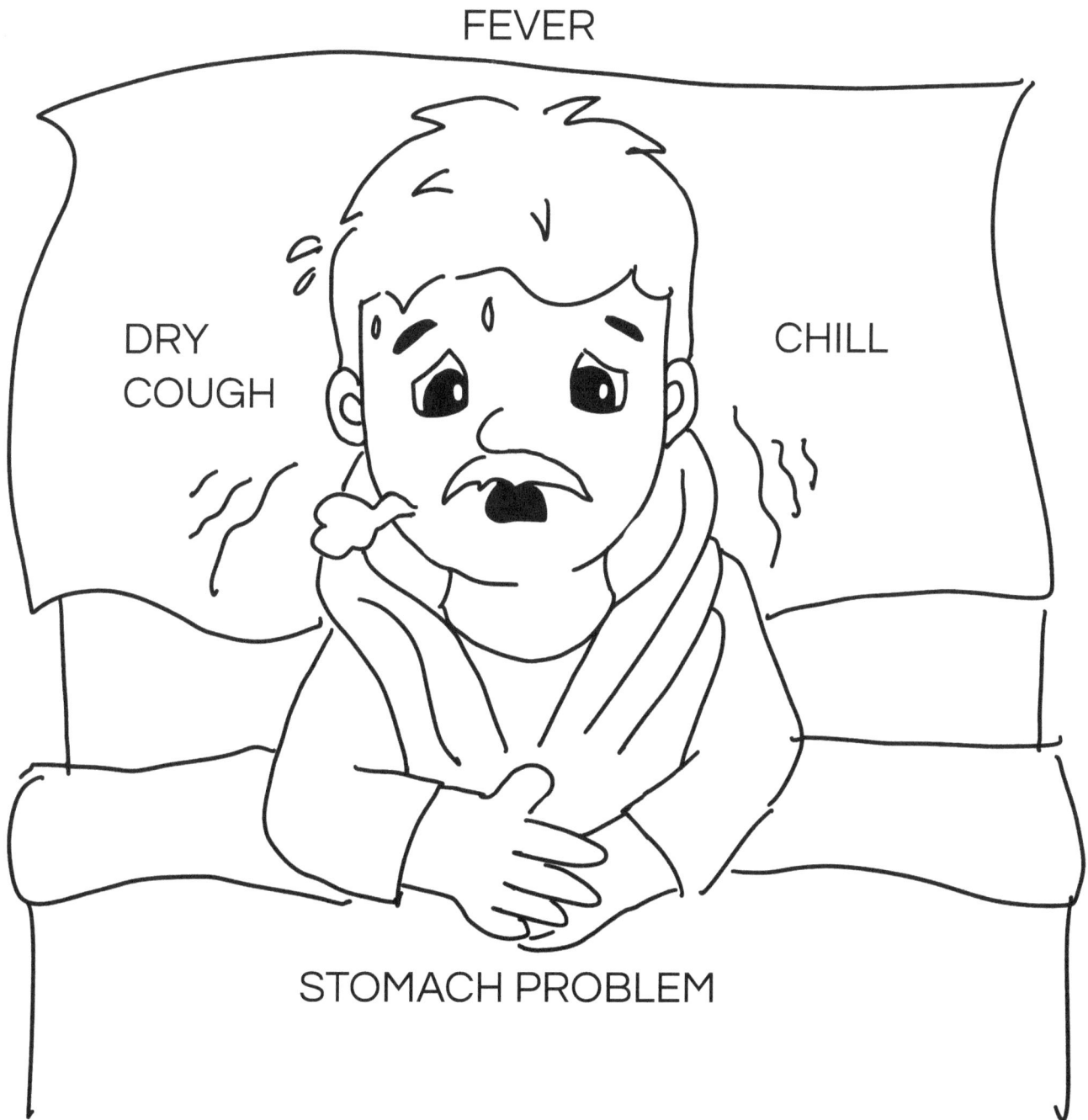

FEVER

DRY
COUGH

CHILL

STOMACH PROBLEM

"Uncle Mike has symptoms similar to a bad cold. He will probably recover - most people do - but Aunt Shari will have to make sure he doesn't get seriously sick or needs to go to the hospital," responded Mom.

Mom looked worried. Dad gave her a big hug and said, "We have great doctors and nurses. We don't have to worry."

Liam asked, "We saw them a week ago, but I don't feel sick. Does this mean we didn't get the virus?"

Daddy explained, "When the microscopic virus enters the body, it could live inside for up to fourteen days before we see symptoms. Some people never get symptoms, but they are still contagious. Since we saw Uncle Mike seven days ago, we have to self-quarantine for another seven days just to be safe. We need to protect ourselves and others."

Liam asked, "How do we make sure we don't get sick?"

"Umm brother!" Livy said eagerly, "We have to be Virus Busters by eating a Rainbow Diet and staying hydrated!"

Mommy giggled and replied,
"Those are a few of the things
Virus Busters do.

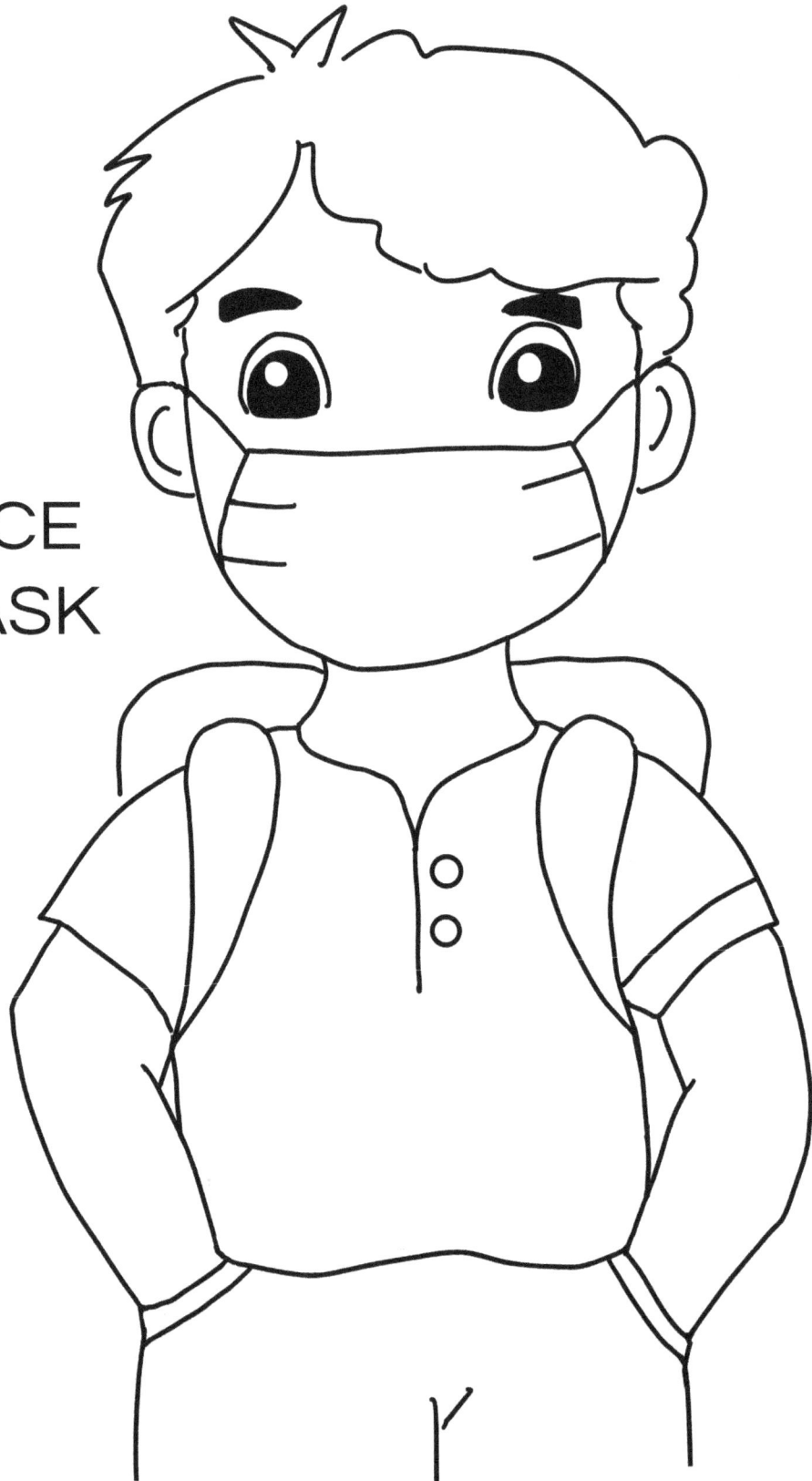

Mommy added, "We need to do more. We need to stop the spread of the virus by making sure we wear a face mask when we are outside.

FACE
MASK

When outside, we need to stay 6 feet or more away from anyone who doesn't live with us. When we see people coming too close, we could walk to an open space and wait until they pass by before we continue."

6 FEET

Mommy continued, "Virus Busters wash their hands for twenty seconds or more with soap and warm water.

20 Seconds

Also, Virus Busters don't touch their faces or play with masks."

Livy whispered, "What if we can't wash our hands?"

No Soap?

No Water?

Liam shouted, "SANITIZER! Mommy already told you to carry it wherever you go!"

Daddy interjected, "There is a lot of information to remember. Livy, you said we are 'Virus Busters,' and we have to do our part by staying away from others. We may be okay, but others can get really sick. We need to work together. We are *not staying home forever;* it is temporary until doctors and scientists find a treatment."

Livy asked, "But what can we do while we are social distancing?"

Daddy replied, "Sweetie, we can still have fun. We can video conference. We can plant a vegetable garden, learn to draw, write stories, and ride our bikes."

Mommy chimed in, "If we miss our cousins, we can see them from a distance while wearing a mask."

"Hi Uncle Mike, we are so glad you called. Everyone is worried about you. Do you have an update?" said Mommy.

buzz....buzz...

Uncle Mike sadly replied, "I tested positive for Covid-19. I am sorry! You need to self-quarantine for seven days."

"Don't worry Uncle Mike, we will because we are the Virus Busters. We will stop the spread." said Livy.

"Don't forget to eat a Rainbow Diet and wash your hands all the time!"

Uncle Mike sincerely responded, "We will be Virus Busters too. Thank you and get plenty of rest."

After Uncle Mike hung up, Liam, Livy, Mommy, and Daddy gave each other a great big family bear hug. "We will get through this," whispered Daddy.

Livy is going to meet a friend at the park. Draw a properly-fitted face mask on Livy.

Liam is going to the beach with his cousin. Draw a properly-fitted face mask on Liam.

HANDWASHING SONG

Complete the lyrics with the words in the box. The tune to the song is Row, Row, Row Your Boat.

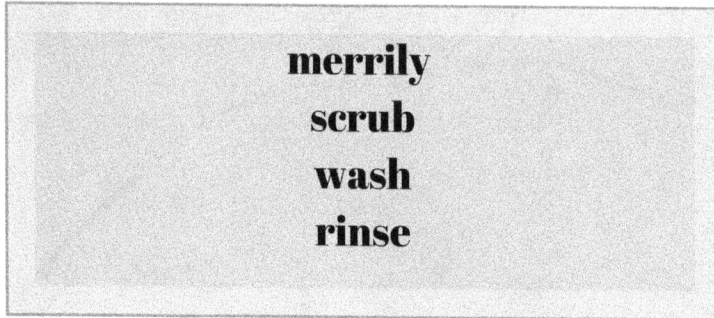

> **merrily**
> **scrub**
> **wash**
> **rinse**

Wash, wash , _____ your hands,

Just like big kids do.

Merrily, merrily, merrily, _____

Add a dab of soap for you.

Scrub, scrub , _____ your hands

Scrub the germs away

Rinse and rinse and rinse and _____

Rinse your hands always

NAME _____ DATE _____

I CAN . . .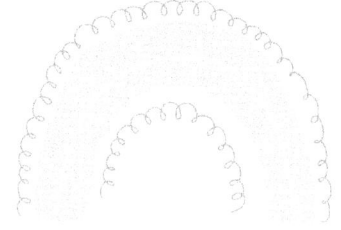

Draw and write three activities you can do during this pandemic.

1._____

_____

_____

_____

2._____

_____

_____

_____

3._____

_____

_____

_____

I can & I will

DRAW
PICTURES OF
YOUR FAVORITE
ACTIVITIES

Draw a picture of your hero.

MY HERO

MY HERO

ALL SET TO WRITE A SUMMARY?

Who is your hero? Support your opinion with details.

_____

_____

_____

_____

_____

_____

_____

_____

_____

_____

Rate My Writing

A Book Review

NAME

DATE

Background and qualifications of the author

The five things I learned:

_____

_____

_____

_____

_____

The target audience

I give this book:

Explanation for rating:

Dear Readers,

Thank you for reading Livy and Liam the Virus Busters. I hope you enjoyed the story with your child. Please consider leaving a review on Amazon, Goodreads, and Google. Reviews help other readers when they are searching for books they might enjoy too.

Thank you
Czarina T-Bernett

Other books by the author!

www.ingramcontent.com/pod-product-compliance
Lightning Source LLC
Chambersburg PA
CBHW081243020426
42331CB00013B/3284